For My Wife,
Rachel
Without Whose Encouragement
This Story Would Not Exist

Dedicted to the Memory
Of a Good Friend,
Sam Robins

Text, Illustrations, & Design ©1998 by Humbug Publishing, L.L.C.
All Rights Reserved
"Humbug" and "A Humbug Christmas" are registered trademarks.
Published by Humbug Publishing, L.L.C.
P. O. Box 10043
Kansas City, MO 64171
Illustrated by Betty Reichmeier
Color Illustration Work by Ronda Krum

A special thanks to Karla & Greg Schiller, the entire Gee Family
Eve Perkal, Nina & Maurice Fraley, The Tiny Bear Lady; Karen Kunst
and the countless others who have helped in so many ways.

Printed by Tien Wah Press

Visit the Humbug at: w w w . h u m b u g s . c o m

ISBN: 0-913751-75-8

Printed in Singapore

A HUMBUG CHRISTMAS

WRITTEN BY TOBIN FRALEY

ILLUSTRATIONS BY
BETTY REICHMEIER

One cold and bleak December day
A year or so ago,
A winter's storm blew from the north
With icy winds and snow.

That night, the children, Tess and I
    Were trapped within our house.
Amanda whined and Billy squirmed,
    Both kids began to grouse.

Three more days 'til Christmas eve,
    Our tree was up and lit,
The presents all were neatly wrapped,
    We'd finished every bit.

"What should we do?" I asked my wife.
At last Tess said, "I know.
I'll make some snacks, and then we'll watch
Our favorite Christmas show."

A Christmas Carol came to life
Upon our TV screen.
The old one with Alastair Sim
As Scrooge, the tight and mean.

We sat entranced by this quaint film
With characters we knew;
Bob Cratchett, Tim, old Marley's ghost,
And Scrooge's poor nephew.

Then came that phrase, that famous line,
    When Scrooge was wished good cheer.
"Bah, HUMBUG!," was his swift reply,
    "Now go, get out of here!"

The moment Scrooge had said those words
    There came a small bright flash,
A puff of smoke, a gust of wind,
    Then from our tree, a crash.

I went to check the Christmas tree
And saw our tabby cat.
A broken glass ball ornament
Lay near to where he sat.

"Bad cat!" said I, with angry voice,
A gruff and grumbly scold.
"One more like that my furry friend,
And you're out in the cold."

Our kitty gave me not a glance
And would not heed my plea,
But stared, transfixed, at something there,
Just underneath the tree.

Yet when I looked to where he gazed,
A sound came from nearby.
It was a kind of giggling laugh,
Then something caught my eye.

I saw a most amazing sight,
For there upon the rug,
Wedged in between two presents was
The oddest looking bug.

He wore a coat and large white gloves,
Big shoes and dapper vest,
Striped stockings covered both his legs,
Gold buttons up his chest.

When he knew that I'd spotted him,
He took off in a flash,
With two big double somersaults,
Then up the tree did dash.

I looked and looked, all through the tree,
Searched branches high and low,
But nowhere was that little bug,
I said, "Where could he go?"

"What's that you said?" Tess called to me,
My head still in a daze.
"Uh, nothing dear, it's just the cat,
He's going through a phase."

Next morning it was bright and clear
I hopped right out of bed.
"Those visions in our Christmas tree,
I must have dreamt," I said.

But when I reached the living room
And opened up the door,
Our Christmas lights lay all around
Spread out across the floor.

At first I didn't understand
What could have happened here,
But then, I thought, last night, of course,
That BUG! It all came clear.

I shovelled snow most of that day,
And then I fixed the tree.
But as I did, thoughts of that bug
Kept coming back to me.

When evening came, I checked each branch
    Before going to bed.
I found no sign of that strange bug,
    Thinking he must have fled.

                I tossed and turned throughout that night,
                    'Til it was light outside,
                Then rubbed my eyes, put on my robe,
                    My mind preoccupied.

Just then the kids came running in
To tell us, "Come and see,
You won't believe what's happened now,
The tinsel's off the tree."

We hurried off to view the scene,
Indeed it was complete,
For all the silver tinsel now
Lay strewn about our feet.

"What could've caused this?" Billy asked.
I dared not say a word.
For who'd believe some bug's to blame.
It sounded so absurd.

I searched each corner of our house.
The bug had left no trace.
I knew I'd have to wait 'til dark
To find his hiding place.

So, carefully I wound the clock,
    Set the alarm for three.
Then placed it 'neath my pillow
    So no one would wake but me.

            Just as I planned, I woke at three
                And slipped out of my bed.
            Then as I tip-toed down the hall,
                A sound came from ahead.

                    I held my breath and listened close,
                        Some music I could hear.
                    A song of sorts, a silly one,
                        From somewhere very near.

Diddlely-Doo, Diddlely-Dee,
I Am A Humbug, Humbug's Me.
Making Mischief In A Christmas Tree,
Schmiddledy-Schmoo, Schmiddledy-Schmee.

Drop An Ornament, Hear It Go Splat,
And Blame It On A Silly Old Cat

Widdlely-Woo, Widdlely-Wee,
I Am A Humbug, Humbug's Me.
Making Mischief In A Christmas Tree,
Fiddledy-Foo, Fiddledy-Fee.

Colored Lights Are Always Too Hot
Unscrew Them All And Then They're Not

Middlely-Moo, Middlely-Mee,
I Am A Humbug, Humbug's Me.
Making Mischief In A Christmas Tree,
Tiddledy-Too, Tiddledy-Tee.

All That Tinsel Makes Me Sneeze
So I Take It Off Of The Christmas Trees.

I Am A Humbug, Humbug's Me.

What made this odd song stranger still
    Was in between each verse,
I heard a kind of munching sound,
    Which made the song much worse.

        At last, I knew the time had come
            To catch him by surprise,
        I flipped the switch, it was too bright
            I had to squint my eyes.

                One quick step back "Oops, there's the cat!"
                    A spin, and then a jump.
                I tripped over my own two feet,
                    And landed with a thump.

The bug was gone, he'd disappeared,
Almost into thin air,
And when I looked around the room
Popcorn was everywhere.

Oh no, I thought, that munching noise,
The one I'd heard before.
He'd eaten all our popcorn strings
And would have eaten more.

The ruckus woke the kids and Tess
They all came in to see
Me sitting there upon the floor
Amidst all the debris.

We gathered 'round the Christmas tree
    Our spirits at a low.
"What's happening?" Amanda sighed.
    At last, I said, "I know."

I told them of the little bug
    And of his serenade,
His purple vest and great big shoes,
    And all the tricks he played.

Then to the kids, Tess said, "Your Dad,
    He's not himself today,
So let's all just go back to bed,
    I'm sure he'll be okay."

They turned to go, I said, "Hey wait,
    There's nothing wrong with me.
This Humbug really does exist.
    I'll catch him, then you'll see."

That day I drilled and sawed and glued,
    And when the evening came,
I'd made a perfect foolproof trap
    To end this Humbug's game.

                With all asleep and in their beds
                    I settled in my chair.
                Alert, awake and ready now,
                    That Humbug I would snare.

The next thing I remember was
    The kids upon my lap
"Wake up," they said, "it's Christmas day,
    No time to take a nap."

        I sat up straight and blinked my eyes
            Then realized with woe,
        I'd missed that Humbug once again.
            Then cried, "THE TREE, OH-NO!"

I focused on our Christmas tree
    Expecting all the worst,
But what I saw, I must admit,
    Caught me off guard at first.

No ornament was out of place,
    The presents all still there.
Each colored light was brightly lit,
    The tinsel hung with care.

Yet overnight the tree had changed,
    Each branch now danced with light.
The room filled with a magic glow,
    A truly wondrous sight.

We stood in awe that Christmas day,
When something else I spied,
Four tiny gifts hung from a branch
Wrapped up and neatly tied.

On each small box a name appeared
In writing neat and trim,
Amanda's, Billy's, Tess' and mine.
I knew they were from him.

In Billy's box, a silver coin,
A magic one it seems,
For when he tossed it in the air,
It glistened like moonbeams.

Amanda's held the smallest bear,
Dressed like a tiny clown,
With golden fur as soft as silk,
And eyes of deepest brown.

"Oh my!" said Tess unwrapping hers,
"I can't believe it's true,
This bracelet, lost ten years ago,
Was my first gift from you."

"What's your gift, Dad?" Amanda asked
    "Let's take a look," I said.
We opened it, I peeked inside,
    Then slowly shook my head.

For in that box, an ornament
    That meant so much to me.
An angel I'd loved as a boy,
    Upon my grandma's tree.

That day our lives were filled with joy
The only wish I had,
Was that my children trust my words
Believing their old Dad.

Just then a card dropped from a branch
I caught it in midair.
And read aloud to everyone
The greeting written there;

To all of you, thanks for the fun,
Be well and have good cheer,
With Humbug blessings on your home,
I'll see you all next year.

H.B.